If It Fits, I Sits

Don't bother me till spring.

G

Gallery Books
An Imprint of Simon & Schuster, Inc.
1230 Avenue of the Americas
New York, NY 10020

Published by arrangement with
The Orion Publishing Group Limited
Originally published in Great Britain
in 2015 by Orion

First Gallery Books hardcover edition May 2016

For information about special discounts for bulk purchases, please contact Simon & Schuster Special Sales at 1-866-506-1949 or business@simonandschuster.com.

The Simon & Schuster Speakers Bureau can bring authors to your live event. For more information or to book an event, contact the Simon & Schuster Speakers Bureau at 1-866-248-3049 or visit our website at www.simonspeakers.com.

Manufactured in the United States of America

10 9 8 7 6 5 4 3 2 1

ISBN 978-1-5011-3422-7
ISBN 978-1-5011-3423-4 (ebook)

If It Fits, I Sits

Cats in Awkward Places

GALLERY BOOKS

New York London Toronto Sydney New Delhi

Actually, these boots were made for snuggling.

You've no idea the day I've had.

I didn't choose the thug life—the thug life chose me.

If you insist on putting treats in weird places, don't be surprised about finding me in weird places.

I'm not sure how this happened, but please just help.

Impeding your gardening is my Zen.

The waffle fur effect is totally in.

Have you tried turning it off and on again?

Library, pleeeaaase . . .

This is just my resting bitch face.

Why so much money and food down here?!

These are not the kitties you're looking for . . .

You're terribly grouchy without coffee.

How am I going to get out of here with no curtains to climb up?

You don't need to open the blinds. You have me to look at.

File me under "S" for sleeping.

You don't need
this, right?

Too-small boxes are the best kind of boxes.

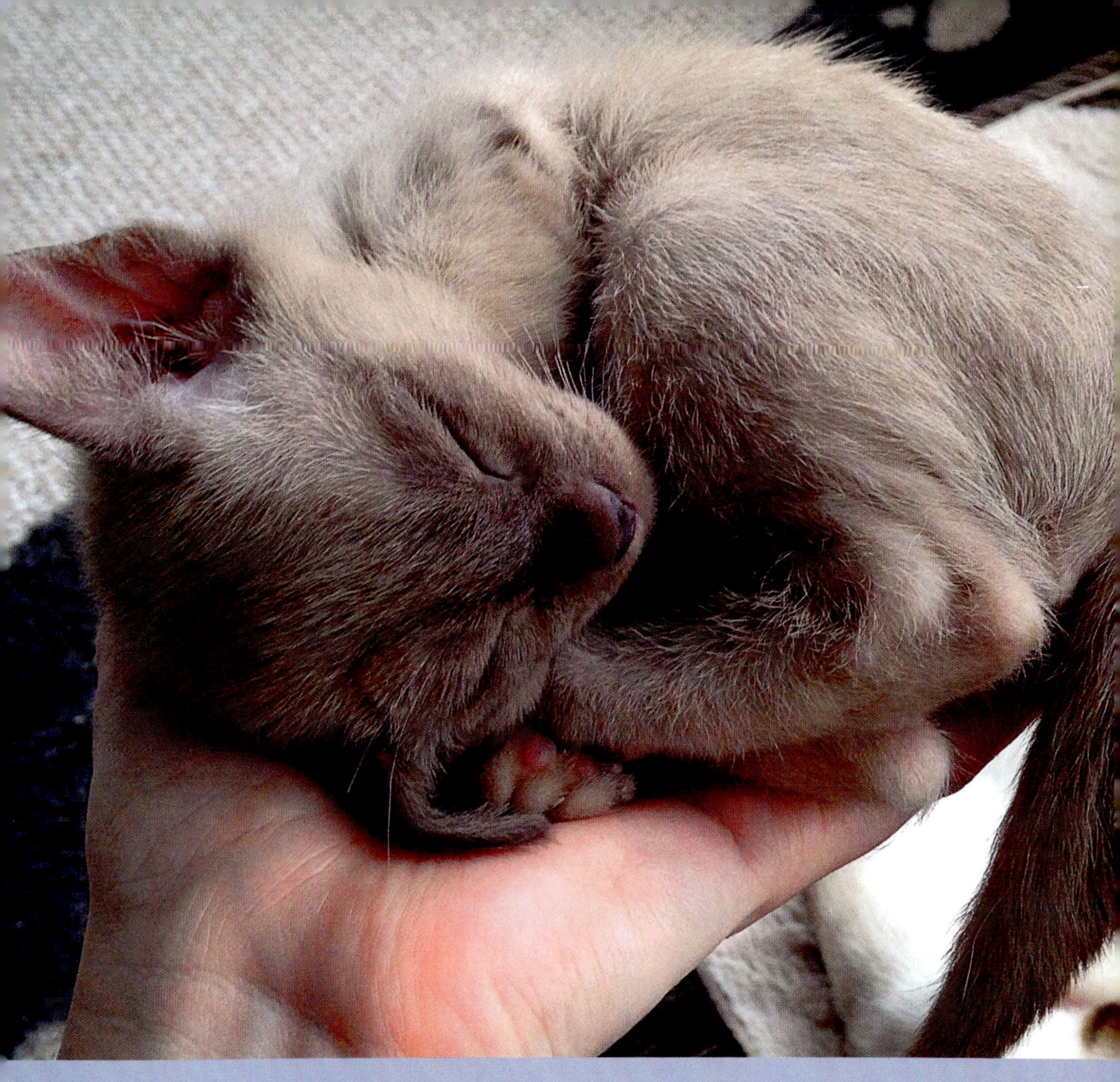

Just hold me.

So . . . someone ate your lunch.

Yeah, I can see your problem back here—cat hair everywhere.

If I'm not supposed to sit here, why so warm?

This is the only time your socks are approachable, so I'm making the most of it.

Baddest Jedi in three galaxies.

Whaaaat? You used it this *morning*!

This didn't go with those shoes anyway.

Physics be damned.

So you found the hideout, but do you know the password?

Oh, a *bird* house, you say?

Get off the *what* now?

Oh, hi.

We're cats. Of *course* we're secretly judging you.

I may not be comfortable, but I *won*.

You . . . might need to run this again.

Living on the edge is exhausting.

Purrrfect.

No is Automatic Treat Machine?

'Twas no dream . . .

You'll call him later.

Why is this force field?!

That did not go as planned . . .

Ground so far!

You're more interesting from up here.

Where are we going?

I think your printer's jammed.

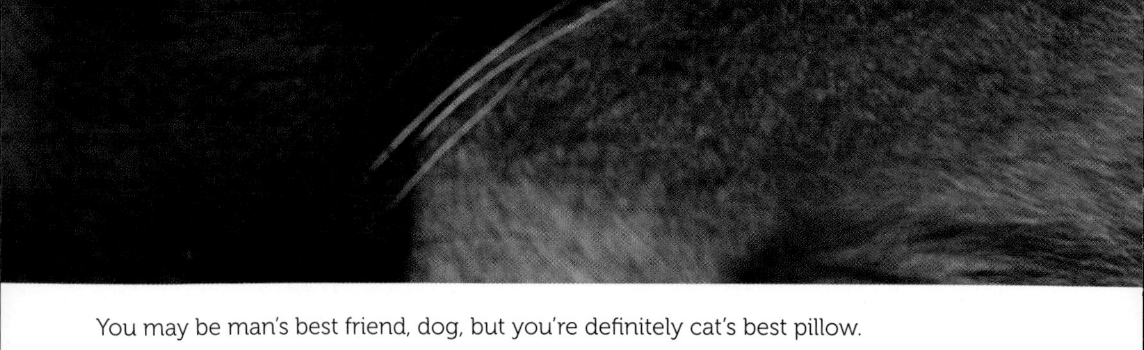

You may be man's best friend, dog, but you're definitely cat's best pillow.

Can I see this in a smaller size?

I told him it was too matchy-matchy.

I have no idea where I am . . . but it's warm.

Are you implying I'm too large for one chair?

Gravity? Bah!

I warned you I'd shrink.

Well, this is embarrassing . . .

As comfy as ever.

Hello there.

I still fit!

Oh, you're still here?

I, Vasco da Gato, first intrepid explorer of the splendid poly-blend caves of North America . . .

Hurry up and hang the decorations. I need my piñata.

You rang?

Wait, is this your paw or mine?

Human dare approach . . .
Ghost cat!?

So much handbag, so
few treats.

You expected Easter eggs, maybe?

I'll admit the creaking sounds are worrying me.

Best sunbathing spot ever!

You're being audited.

I've been to better spas, to be honest.

"Some assembly required"? No—shut up!

If I dream hard enough, these will be yarn . . .

Where. Are. The. Cat. Books.

Believe it or not, I planned this.

Yes, I see: back-to-back tickles under the chin with me all afternoon.

What're *you* looking at? I see you sneaking in here at night!

Come at me, winter.

I don't have to explain anything to you.

One more hour
and the birds will
trust me.

Someday so fluffy
I fill this bag . . .

No open the box? No more box.

I tried to sit . . . something went wrong.

If I fall, this couch is in *big* trouble.

Where was this when I got stuck in that tree all afternoon?!

Who needs fruit?

Think he knows I'm here?

Chill. Your plants will be fine.

I'll try not to snag all your tights with my claws, but I can't promise anything.

A fine chariot. For once, you have done well.

A) Immerse self in classics.
B) Cough up hair ball.

Let's face it . . . you're never going to read all these.

Hey! Need a bookmark?

You got me loft apartment?

Did you just say "hubcats"? Oh, wow.

Did someone call an Uber?

All I need is guitar lessons. And thumbs.

Worship me.

Find your own bowl to sit in.

The comfort of being here only just outweighs the smell.

Just tell me where the treats are.

One . . . more . . . inch . . .

Leave me alone: my Cirque du Soleil audition is tomorrow.

Soon, human.

I'm fast *and* furrrious.

Mmmm . . . boooOxxxx.

Minipimer

Up seemed easier . . .

Fancy a spot of tea?

I will not rest until I am perfectly circular.

I fit. What's the problem?

The secret to comfort actually lies in this outstretched paw.

Someone's been scratching the DVDs?!

You're going to need a lot more than just ambition.

Might be stuck here awhile. Not sure yet.

Crazy like a *cat*!

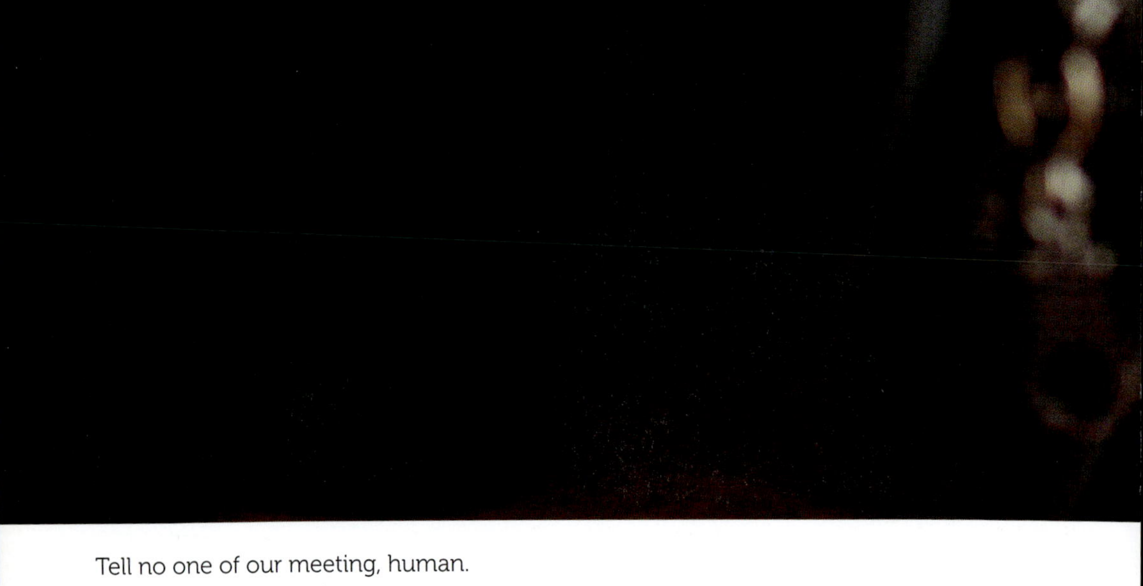

Tell no one of our meeting, human.

The best thing about plastic crates is this little bit where I can rest a tiny part of my face.

Another shopping trip, still no ham. I'm not angry, I'm just plotting my revenge.

When my paws unfreeze, I'm coming for you.

"Use it as a toboggan," they said. "We'll come get you," they said . . .

Forget your nativity.
I'm the star.

If you could just keep getting bigger shoes as I grow, that'd be great.

Downward Dog is out.
Scrambled Cat is in.

Sorry, no room here. You're going to have to take the floor.

Picture credits

DaLy/Shutterstock

Wilson Pickett
Emily Smith

Lena Lir/Shutterstock

Agata Dorobek/ Shutterstock

Eric Cantona
Adele Pullarp

Maksymowicz/iStock

Boris
Henry Hemming

ivanoffotography/ Shutterstock

fzd.it/Shutterstock

BettinaSampl/iStock

apolonia/Shutterstock

Caxton
Chris Stork

Maurizio Cefano/ 19Cefa94/Flickr/ Creative Commons

Loki
Rebekah Davies

The Len/Shutterstock

Hanzi-mor/ Shutterstock

anurakpong/iStock

MaxyM/Shutterstock

Renata Osinska/ Shutterstock

Valeri Potapova/ Shutterstock

ferrerivideo/iStock

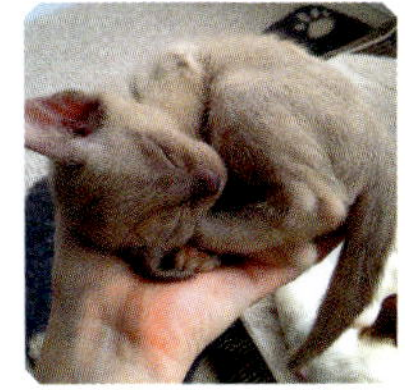

ahloch/iStock

uccia_photography/ Getty

Benoit Daoust/ Shutterstock

Eugenio Marongiu/ Shutterstock

Sari O'Neal/ Shutterstock

valiooo/iStock

Belle *BoulderPhoto/Shutterstock*

Bezzangi/Shutterstock

bigworld/iStock

In Tune/Shutterstock

ian35mm/iStock

volcank/iStock

OndagoArts/iStock

Aubord Dulac/ Shutterstock

DeltaOFF/iStock

BettinaSampl/iStock

Zanna Holstova/ Shutterstock

Nataliya Kuznetsova/ Shutterstock

Avangard Photography/ Shutterstock

PawelG Photo/ Shutterstock

Anna Jurkovska/ Shutterstock

apeyron/Shutterstock

Pidgoma Levgeniia/ Shutterstock

mzamur/iStock

Malibu
Giuliana Heatherington

Malibu
Giuliana Heatherington

Gato
Mercedes Basso

Valentina Razumova/ Shutterstock

Bela
Duncan Millar & Francisco Oliveira

Zanna Holstova/ Shutterstock

Edinorog/iStock

Fannie/*Autumn Barnes/ autbarnes08/Flickr/ Creative Commons*

mugensx/iStock

Andrey_Kuzmin/ Shutterstock

MaxyM/Shutterstock

Frankieleon/Flickr/ Creative Commons

Sylvia sooyoN/ Shutterstock

Herbie
Cathryn Gilbert

Rappholdt/Shutterstock

fotata/Shutterstock

ivz/iStock

Joanna Zaleska/iStock

FooTToo/iStock

Nadinelle/Shutterstock

Pebbles
Alex Pidduck

John Ruskin
Marta Owzcarek

Kichigin/Shutterstock

olcha/Shutterstock

Brutus
Annie Martin

Claude
Kimberly Washford

DreamBig/Shutterstock

Zanna Holstova/ Shutterstock

Marlinde/Shutterstock

Manja/Shutterstock

Gail Johnson/ Shutterstock

horvathta/Shutterstock

IrinaK/Shutterstock

Koldunov Alexey/ Shutterstock

Mac99/iStock

cip1000/iStock

Ben
Pat Bland

Lovely
Lisa Milton

wideshuts/Shutterstock

liveostockimages/iStock

Tinks
Rebecca Sharman

wolfman57/Shutterstock

dogi/Shutterstock

Photoseeker/Shutterstock

Francesca Yorke/Getty

Steve
CaptMikey9/Flickr/Creative Commons

Phooey/iStock

Charlie
David Bamford

DaLy/Shutterstock

Nutmeg
Lucie Stericker

epicurean/iStock

NicO_l/Shutterstock

mariakbell/iStock

fiorigianluigi/iStock

ThomasShanahan/iStock

Evgeny Sergeev/iStock

Benoit Daoust/Shutterstock

Nadinelle/Shutterstock

Viesinsh/iStock

John Ruskin
Marta Owzcarek

Anna Jurkovska/Shutterstock

Mouse
Suzie Doore

Neil
Sebastian Rydberg

Sitikka/iStock

soulrebel83/iStock

ferrerivideo/iStock

Meoita/Shutterstock

Waffle
Amanda Jones

Smokey Joe
Anna Valentine

Vampirica/iStock

mrak_hr/iStock

Vampirica/iStock

paranoix/iStock

Max
Judy Gee

Karl Umbriaco/ Shutterstock

vvvita/iStock

Jesus Christ
Natasha Vouckelatou

Belle
Amanda Thursby

Zhenikeyev/iStock

Monty
Charlotte Morris